A
Log Cabin Notebook

by
Mary Ellen Hopkins

This book is dedicated to my mother, Vivian Ewing Ingle.

Mary Ellen Hopkins
Santa Monica, CA
Vivian's Quilt
(found on page 34)

Table of Contents

Mary Ellen Hopkins
Santa Monica, CA
Cover Quilt
(found on page 50)

The Log Cabin Block

I put this block into first place years ago and it has NEVER been bumped from that spot.

You could easily dedicate your entire quilting life to this block and never repeat yourself.

Top of the list for versatility! Graphic designs, pictorials, just plain fabric shadings – all these can be interpreted using Log Cabin blocks. Hopefully, this "Notebook" will open your eyes to some new approaches.

CHECK OUT YOUR EQUIPMENT

An Olfa mat and rotary cutter, with a Salem rule are almost a must. Moving your ironing station close by, having a TV in front of you, and getting a looooong phone cord make the quality of life better.

Deluxe extras: 5" Ginghers with your initials engraved; a revolving, rolling secretarial chair; BIG foam-core board covered with batting, available at any art supply store; large see-through sweater boxes, a separate one for each different size cut strip.

And TOP of the Heap, Queen of the Hill – a real sewing table, the kind your sewing machine fits down into.

Even if you're a die-hard hand quilter, do consider machine quilting these Log Cabins – there are so MANY seams to go over!

Yardage is always more than you think. Best bet is to buy long. I can tell you that a double bed size log cabin, cut 1½" takes:

  5 yards total of darks (could be 10 different ½ yards)
  5 yards total of lights (could be 10 different ½ yards)
  ½ yard for center squares. There will be enough left over
  to add a 1½" cut first border all around.

The Author's Personal Rules

Quilters have always had fiercely independent streaks buried beneath their serene outsides – and this block seems to bring out this streak more than any other.

So..... Read my rules, read other quilters' rules, make up some of your own, pick and choose and you'll soon have your own personal and adamant set of rules.

1. I never, ever cut my strips wider than 1½" (finished size 1" or less.)

    I prefer strips that are cut 1¼" (finished size ¾" or less.)

2. Blocks should be small – 6" best – (sometimes maybe 7".) Your design will repeat more and therefore seem twice as intricate.

3. I prefer the block mainly dark, rather than half light and half dark:

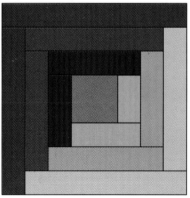

Traditional
half light, half dark
Start with light strip, end with dark strip.

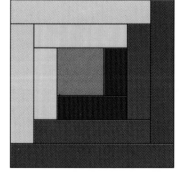

Mainly Dark
Start with dark strip, end with dark strip.

4. The quilting all too often gets overlooked. I'm speaking to machine quilters here. First, I ditch all the blocks to get the quilt well anchored down.

    Now, decide on a superimposed quilting design – each quilt will be totally different.

    A. Never say to yourself, "This is enough for the batt!"
    B. Never say to yourself, "I can't superimpose any quilting – the thread will show!"
    C. Remember, circular quilting will be a great relief on all those straight lines you got from the piecing.

Technical Sewing

Notes on Seam Allowances:

There are LOTS of seams in these blocks, so you need to do everything you can to keep these blocks the same size – especially when you're making them over a long period of time. I call a long period anything over two weeks!

The perfect ¼" seam allowance means absolutely nothing – you just need to have a consistent seam allowance. You DO NOT need to know what your seam allowance measures because you are never going to add or subtract it.

If you can see that you are going to make a certain Log Cabin quilt over a long period of time, there is really an outside chance that you may get a NEW SEWING MACHINE half way through, which would change your seam allowance. Therefore, if you have made ALL your round ones at once for every block, and ALL your round twos at once, etc, and THEN, at the beginning of say, round five, you find yourself with a new machine, you are now taking a new seam allowance on every single block. This means every single block is still the same size. (If this has you confused, just take my word for it.)

A sewing table – the kind where your machine sits DOWN INSIDE is definitely more important than a new machine. These tables come in dozens of models and dozens of prices. The plain utilitarian one works just as well as the gorgeous fancy one. Try one for five minutes and you'll understand.

Construction:

STEP 1:   Sew center block strip and first round together.
Press to one side.
Slice off the width of center block strip.

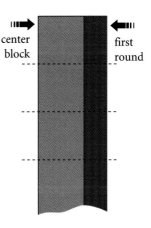

STEP 2: Lay these pieces, right sides together on second round strip, BEING SURE to leave a little space between. This is so when you cut them apart. you're saved from cutting them at an angle.

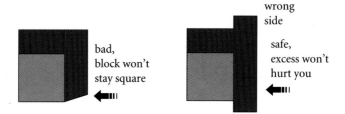

STEP 3: Same as step 2, using the center square edge.

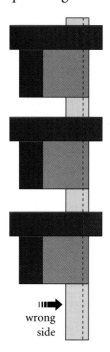

STEP 4: You could sew this round the same as step 3, but I have found it to be more efficient to slice off several strips at one time that are slightly longer than I need and string them through the machine. I do not need to painstakingly line up the top of the strip to the top of the block (which makes me crazy after just a few minutes.) I can slap them down and go....! Press.

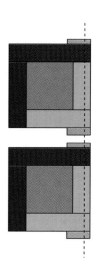

STEPS 5-13: Same as Step 4.

The trick is to keep these blocks SQUARE and pressed flat as a pancake. If all your blocks are exactly the same size, you are indeed an expert! More than likely, they vary a little bit – not to worry – it's all going to work.

ICKY SOLUTION – You could trim all the blocks to the same size – UGH, not fun.

HAPPY SOLUTION – You merely sew the blocks together into two's and four's and keep your normal sunny disposition!

Lay the blocks out in finished positions. Sew all blocks into pairs, always centering the smaller square on the larger square. Sew together, pretending they are both the size of the smaller one.

Now sew into foursies lining up ONLY the center seam – do not pay attention to the outer edges.

Now sew foursies into eightsies lining up ONLY the center seam, always sewing your seam from the smaller block edge.

Carry on – it will be easy because you have averaged out all your block sizes by now. Your outside logs on your blocks will have a slight variation, BUT your quilt will be flat as a pancake and all your block seams will line up perfectly. My quilt on page 15 is a perfect example of this.

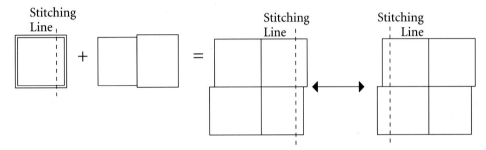

Traditional Variations

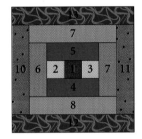

Courthouse Steps

The Chevron Log Cabin

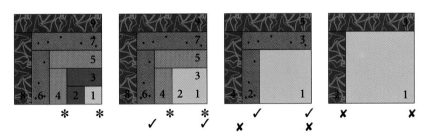

For the Chevron Log Cabin, you build only on two sides of your beginning square, or rectangle. The two quilts pictured on pages 10-11 use blocks with the same size beginning squares. However, as you can see by the four blocks shown here, you can change your beginning square and still have the blocks the same size when finished. Just use your PPM's (Personal Private Measurement). Measure from the star to the star (raw edge) and cut your next beginning square that size. Measure from the check to the check (raw edge) for your next beginning square, then from the x to the x for the next, etc.

Mary Beth Seeley
Brentwood, CA

Note the window-paning is the same as the center square.

Marguerite Lu
Los Angeles, CA

...piecing the back is always fun!

Back of quilt from
previous page.

Rectangular Chevron Log Cabin Grillwork
designed January, 1988

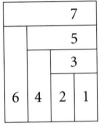
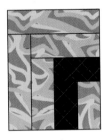
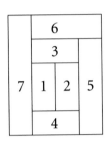

Sewing Order   Color   Sewing Order   Color

Block A   Block B

Four Block A's with
Window-paning

Four Block B's with
Window-paning

The background fabric in Block A and the background fabric in Block B should be similar –
just a subtle difference.

Sew alternate blocks together – remember, this cannot be pieced on the diagonal because the
blocks are not square.

*This is one of my favorite pages.

But, of course if you make the blocks square – you could go on the diagonal.

 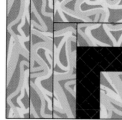  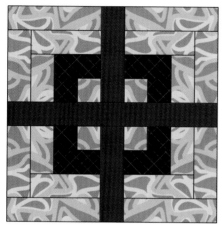

Block A   or   Alternate Block A   Block B   or   Alternate Block B

Four Block A's   Four Block B's

Mary Ellen Hopkins
Santa Monica, CA

Courthouse Steps

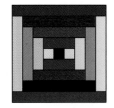

Regular Courthouse Block
Half light
Half dark

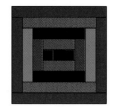

Courthouse Block
All dark

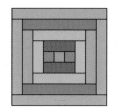

Courthouse Block
All light

This design definitely looked best when put on the diagonal.

The fabrics are all muckled up except in the regular block one fabric is in the same place.

Mary Ellen Hopkins
Santa Monica, CA

Please promise to look at the quilt like this!

Bottom

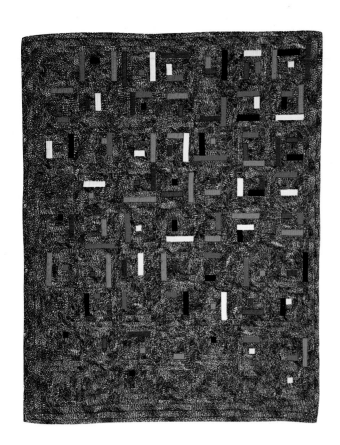

Sally Trude
Santa Monica, CA

Mary Beth Seeley
Brentwood, CA

How to Design

This is as easy as learning to type "A S D F" and "J K L :J" that first day in typing 101. Remember, you could do that without looking!

This lovable block is really just a RIGHT TRIANGLE!!!!

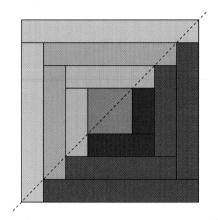 =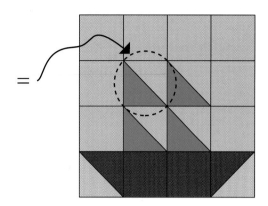

And a SOLID DARK square would be: And a SOLID LIGHT square would be:

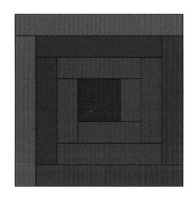   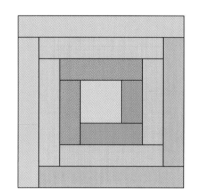

Therefore, the entire *It's Okay If You Sit On My Quilt Book* could be made out of Log Cabin blocks!!!! Or, you could use all Courthouse Steps!

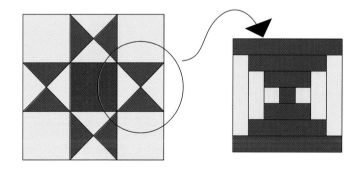

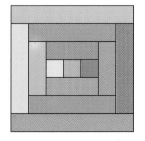   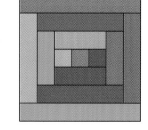

all lights   all mediums

Let's look at a design very carefully. This one is on page 68, #233, "It's Okay..."

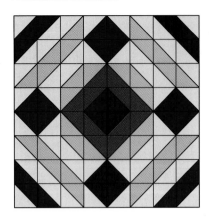

Drawn eight squares across and eight squares down, makes a total of 64 squares. Each square is shown as a right triangle, HOWEVER, we'll interpret each right triangle square as a Log Cabin Block!

There are four basic blocks in this design. They are shown here in their locations.

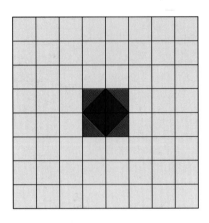
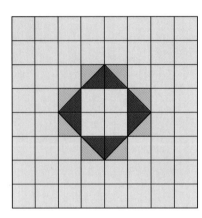
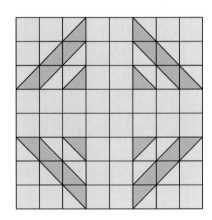

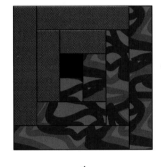
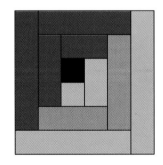
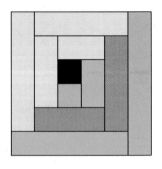

4   8   24

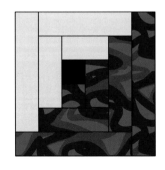

28

Mary Ellen Hopkins
#233, page 68, "It's Okay..."

Night and Noon
#187, page 60, "It's Okay..."

As many of you know, I would rather be making quilts than most anything else, especially after being away on an extended trip! When I arrive home there are grocery sacks of mail to go through, bills to pay....you know what I mean! And, when I am really tired I usually make log cabin blocks. Well, this Night and Noon design came about after one of my extended trips, and because I fell in love with a fuchsia fabric that no one else seemed to know was just wonderful! I feel like the center of #187 is too clunky looking, so I have made it into four log cabin blocks. As I chose the fabrics for this quilt, those who were in the shop at the time thought I was crazy, or at least excessively over tired. BUT, they all came back the next day to see what I had done! Don't forget, YOU DON'T HAVE TO LOVE A FABRIC TO USE IT IN A QUILT! It is very important to use fabrics for the texture and value they offer, not just how beautiful they may be!

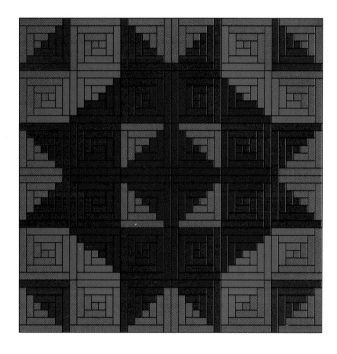

		13				
		9				
		5				
12	8	4	1	2	6	10
		3				
		7				
		11				

"light" side
starts with #2

Mary Ellen Hopkins
Santa Monica, CA

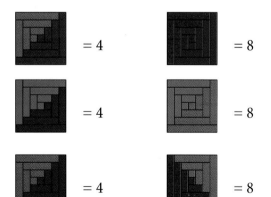

= 4

= 8

= 4

= 8

= 4

= 8

Annette Levey
Marina del Rey, CA
Eddy Stone Light
(seen on page 62, #213, "It's Okay...")

We have Annette to thank for piecing this "teaching" quilt for us. You can see that the top two stars have different corners than the bottom two stars. You can <u>change</u> a pattern to suit yourself.

Log Cabin Basket

(4 patch)

59, page 43, "It's Okay..."

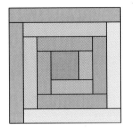 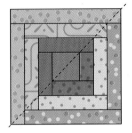  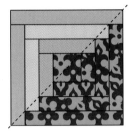

| 5 all light
tiny Log Cabin Blocks | 6 – ½ lights
½ pink
Log Cabin Blocks | 1 all blacks | 4 – ½ lights
½ blacks |

Cut your strips no wider than 1¼".

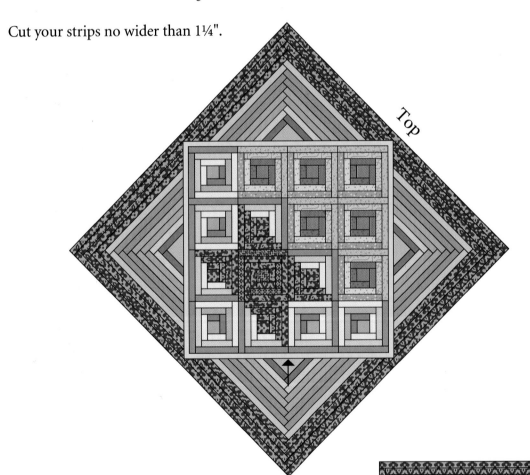

Top

Two of these large log cabin blocks cut in half diagonally finish the sides of your basket. Make them much larger than you think you will need.

22

Jan Krueger
Hales Corners, WI

A faithful reproduction by Jan of Mary Ellen's quilt made in 1984 that has been missing.
(Has since happily returned, but not in time to be photographed for this book.)

Brown Goose – Organized Scrap

#64, page 43, "It's Okay…"

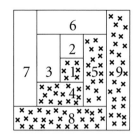

Cut 1¼" wide
Block approximately 4"

This one is a real charmer. But the blocks MUST be kept tiny.

Surprisingly fast and easy (the mind is not over-taxed.) Since all 16 blocks of each little Brown Goose are the same, you can send all 16 of them stringing through at the same time. AUTOMATIC-PILOT-CRUISE CONTROL!

Each brown goose set is made up of muckled up strips of one color family, i.e. Blues & Purples, Reds & Fuchsias.

Each set of 16 blocks should take about six 44" long, 1¼" wide strips of your darks.

Count on at least ⅓ yard worth of darks for each set – for insurance and to use in borders.

Count on at least one yard of background fabric for every four Brown Goose sets. And, yes, of course you can use different, but similar background fabrics.

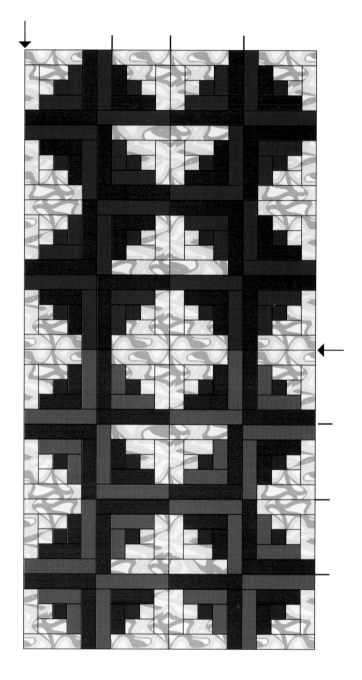

*However, if you want to use that one red, and you're a little short, of course you fill in with a second red. This is a SCRAP quilt!

GREAT NOTE: You could mix in some other 4-patch patterns. You could use them as a border around an 8-patch, or 12-patch, or 16-patch log cabin medallion center. (See page 68, #233, "It's Okay… as a for instance.)

Log Cabin Medallion Star

Some blocks need jazzing up! (You can change a block around any way you want to – remember, you are a snotty, independent American woman!)

The little 4-patch star would be pretty plain and clunky made with 16 Log Cabins.

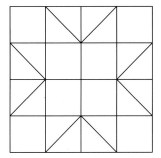

So let's divide the four center blocks into 16 little blocks!

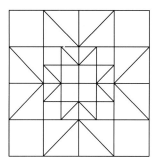

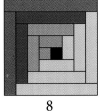

8

Block is 8 strips wide.

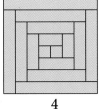

4

Block is 8 strips wide.

8

4

4

Blocks are 4 strips wide.

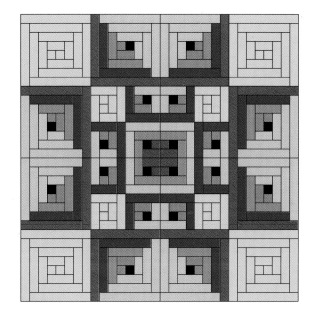

For a center medallion straight or on point.

Best if strips are cut 1¼" wide.

Alone this makes a nice wall hanging or pram quilt.

See pages 37 and 41 also.

Mary Ellen Hopkins
Santa Monica, CA
pieced & quilted, 1979

Design Tricks

"#3: Remember the famous 9-patch set up"

 (from the box of tricks on page 110 or page 2 of the
 "It's Okay..." book depending on when you purchased yours.)

Thought process is as follows:

9-patch = Checkerboard = Red and Black = 2 colors

Let's use two blocks instead of two colors.

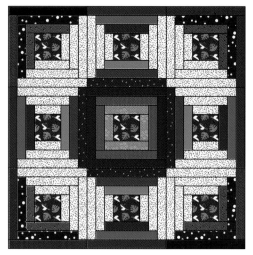

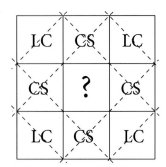

Block #1 will be a Log Cabin.
Block #2 will be a Courthouse Step.

Take another step – we know we'll get even MORE designs from the corners of repeats of the above set. The photo below and on the next page help to illustrate this point.

9-Patch Courthouse Step variation
as seen through the eyes of

Judy Woods
Los Angeles, CA

Mary Ellen Hopkins
Pieced and quilted June, 1986.

Judy Woods
Torrance, CA
Joseph's Coat (now Victorian Navajo)
(seen on page 103, "It's Okay...")

Sunshine and Shadow Variation

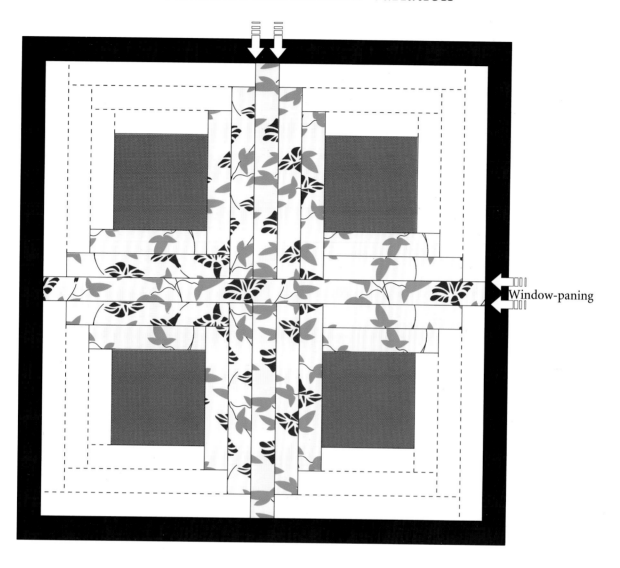

Window-paning

Same fabric in each 4 block set. Note: There must be window--paning between the four blocks.

I suggest cutting the centers 3½" and the strips 1¼"; anything else is just too wide. At this cut size; block is already between 14" and 14¼".

Joan Novack
Detroit, MI

Log Cabin Variation

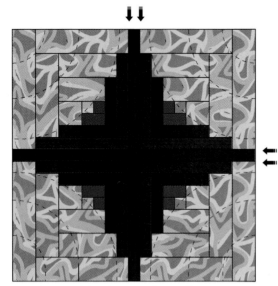

These 4 blocks equal 14¼" square.

Dark strips = ¾", cut 1¼"
Light strips = 1½", cut 2"
Center is light = ¾", cut 1¼"

Quilting is done in curves.

4 x 5 = 20 sets = 57" x 71¼"

Round 1 = ⅓ yard
Round 2 = 1 yard
Round 3 = 1⅓ yards

Window--paning = ¾ yard

Background lights = 2½ yards
Suggest large multi-colored light print.

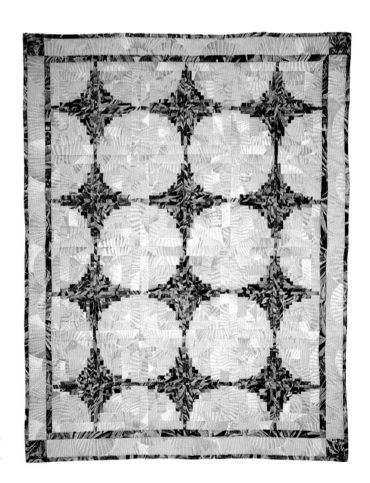

Kathryn Small
Westwood, CA

Barn Raising

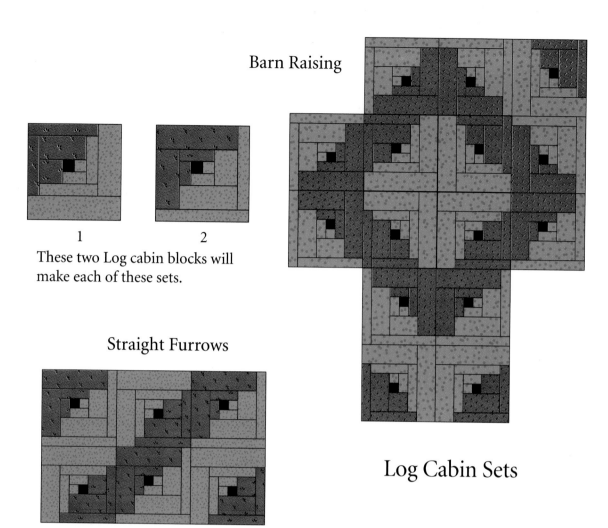

1 **2**

These two Log cabin blocks will make each of these sets.

Straight Furrows

Log Cabin Sets

Sunshine and Shadows

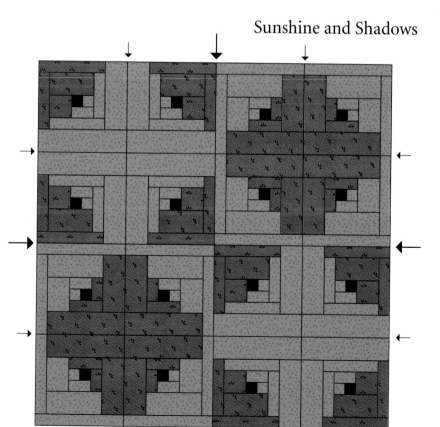

Grid on Top of a Plaid

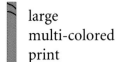

large
multi-colored
print

pale
one-color
print

pale
one-color
print

A
make 68

B
make 72

high contrast
color for "grid"

Cut strips 1¼" wide - block will be approximately 5¼" finished.

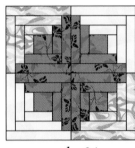

make 24

make 10

make 10

keep 4
for corners

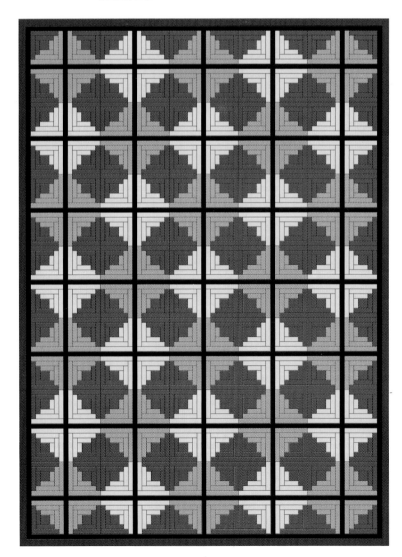

Following the diagram, window-pane these sections with the high contrast strips that are also cut 1¼" wide.

The blocks need to stay about 5¼" – this size will show off the "plaid" nicely. Any larger and the "plaid" will get lost.

To make a quilt the size of the diagram, approximately 61" x 82", you will need:

 3 yards of a large multi-colored print

 1½ yards of #1

 1½ yards of #2

 ½ yard high contrast

Mary Beth Seeley
Brentwood, CA

Mary Ellen Hopkins
Santa Monica, Ca

NOTE: Not enough of a repeat
to see plaid.

Vivian's Quilt – for the Davenport

CENTER

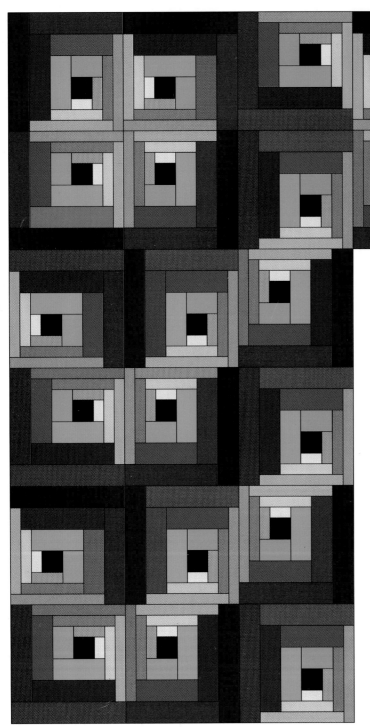

Made as scrap quilt – every log could be different.

Cut lights 1¼" – finished size will be ¾".
Cut darks 1½" – finished size will be 1".

Do not make the dark side all dark – must have some medium-lights mixed in!
The light side of the quilt in the photo is not all that light, either!

When I'm stringing them through, I do four alike each time.

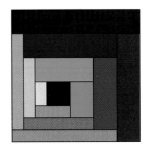

The basic block.

Both quilts shown here
were made by

Barbara Spielberg
Los Angeles, CA
Barn Raising Quilts

Notice how her use of
medium value fabrics
break up the look of solid
dark rings.
(More about this concept
on page 61.)

The Coastal Quilters' Guild Project

When my best friend, Harriet Berk, found out I was writing this book, she asked if she could offer a challenge to her guild. The challenge would be to make a Log Cabin variation from any block in the It's Okay book AND use one or all of my star fabrics in the quilt. When I went to speak to their guild I would judge the quilts and pick ONE for the book.

Well, the challenge was issued, the quilts were made and....when I saw the quilts, I was taken aback at how wonderful they all were. They had taken the simple challenge and gone a few steps beyond!

Of course, my easy decision was immediately impossible. I was supposed to give it at the end of my talk, and all during my talk I had in the back of my mind the nagging question, "Well, what's your choice?" And the nagging response (also in the back of my mind) consisted of a series of "umms," and "ers," followed by "What was the question?"

As I looked out over the crowd while talking, I saw anticipation. And I hoped they wouldn't see me sweat over my consternation. But then, aha! I had a brilliant idea (the proverbial light bulb! Well, at least a refrigerator light!) Why not use them all? THAT was my decision.

After the talk I finally announced that "the quilts are all so gorgeous, I can't decide on one over all the others. So, I'm going to put them all in my book!" I just knew this would be well received. For a moment I saw a look on their faces that said, "No, really, Mary Ellen, which one is it?"

That's my challenge to you: YOU decide. So, I present for your enjoyment and consideration the Star Fabric Log Cabin Challenge Quilts from The Coastal Quilters' Guild.

The basic instructions I gave were as follows:

> I prefer the blocks mainly dark. That means you must start our rounds from the center square with a dark. Then you also end your rounds with a dark. I would NEVER cut the strips wider than 1½" (this should give you a 6" block.) Cuts of 1¼" looks terrific.
>
> Use any pattern from *It's Okay If You Sit On My Quilt*. #233 on page 68 is already done. Sure hope someone wants to do #244 on page 69!! I've also done #187 on page 60, *Night and Noon*, but it's subtle, I don't think it photographs well – so that's a possibility. The four patch basket on page 43 is already done.
>
> I'm so excited about you guys doing this – can hardly wait to see them all.
>
> The blocks don't have to be mainly dark – sometimes it won't work that way. If you need this look – do a Courthouse Steps.

Coastal Quilters' Guild
of
Santa Barbara, CA
presents

Lauren L. Ball
It"s Okay ...To Be Different"

Harriet Berk

Liz Steele

Maggie Godwin
Starry Starry Geese

Sandi Globus
#340, Cathedral Window

Phyliss Peterson
#31 Variation

Pat Yamada
Star Wars

Sally Boden Testa
Don't Fence

Judy Gorrindo
#258, West Virginia

Ellie Wright

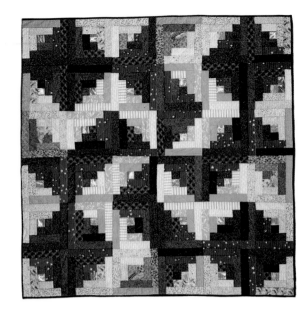

Doris Floyd

Marge Hall
CNN

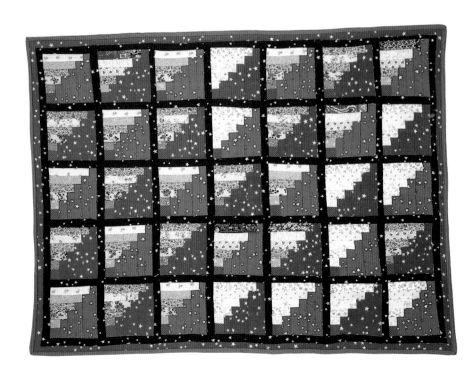

40

Pat Yamada
"I Thought I Followed the Book"

Harriet Berk

Marty Frolli
Abacus

Zetta Hanna
All Purples

Lauren L. Ball
Borealis

Ruth Wolfe's Rainbow Log Cabin Quilt

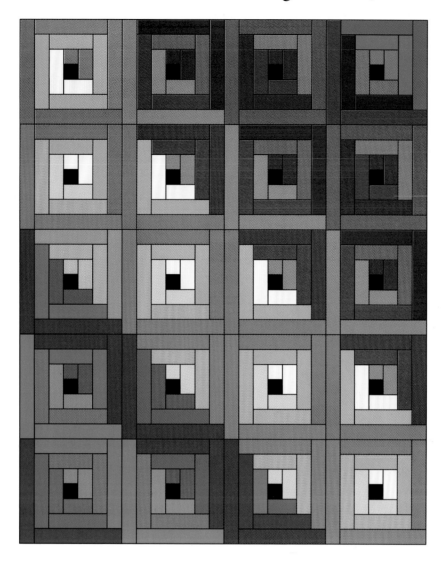

One beautiful rainbow across the quilt is spectacular. This was made with all small prints, different yellows, different reds, etc. Hardest to find will be the orange prints. (Another reason our stashes are color-coordinated!)

Ruth's centers were yellow, but as you can see here, black centers work well also.

No room or board to lay this one out??

…waiiiit a minute! What if each block was a complete rainbow? And you made all the blocks the same?

Think of the possibilities! I'll leave this for you to play with.

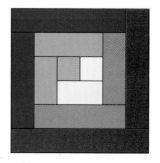

Log Cabin Worksheet #1

designed August 26, 1988

A = 8   B = 9   C = 7   D = 7   E = 4

35 Blocks – Cut 1¼"

Log Cabin Worksheet #2

designed August 26, 1988

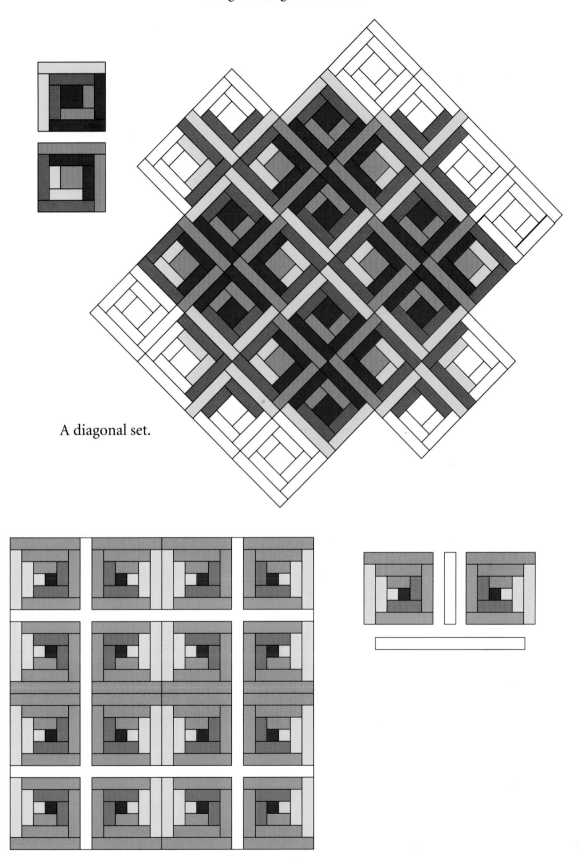

A diagonal set.

Courthouse Steps Worksheet #1
designed August 5, 1988

Rectangle Blocks

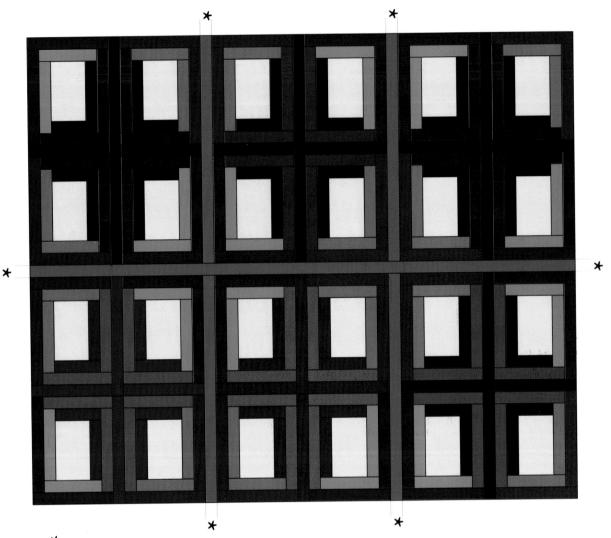

* NOTE Window Paning

Courthouse Steps
Worksheet #2
designed August 26, 1988

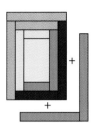

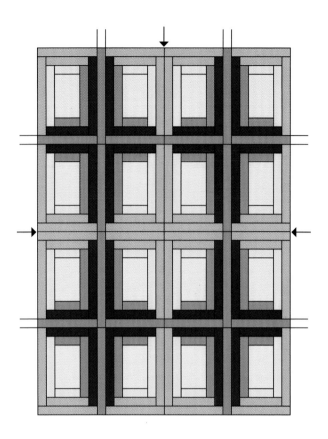

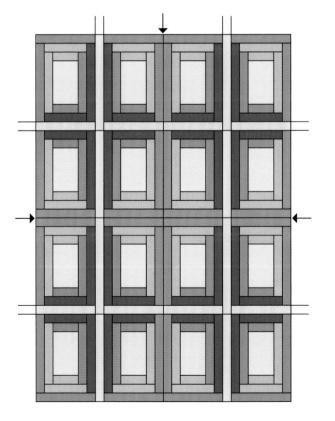

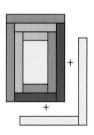

Courthouse Steps Worksheet
Visual Effect is Same Size Squares

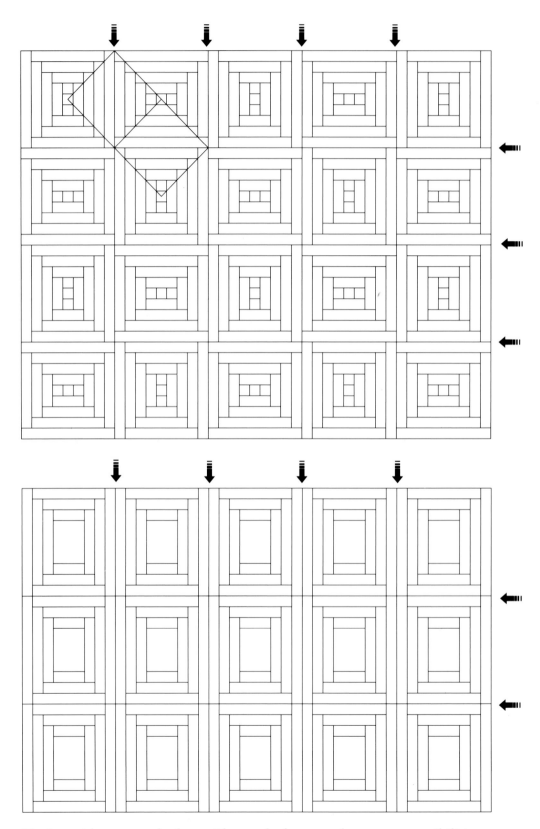

Playing with a rectangle shape. The marked squares have great possibilities.

Courthouse Steps Worksheet
Visual Effect is Different Size Squares

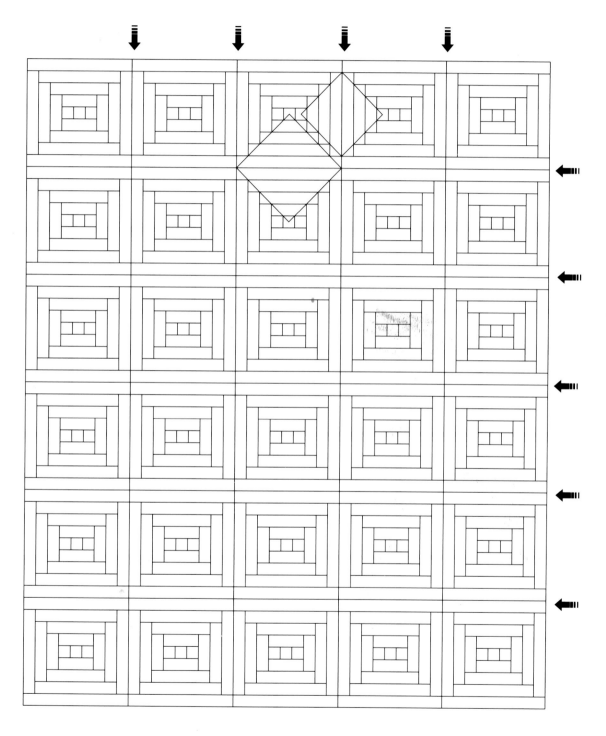

This is the layout of the cover quilt.

Courthouse Steps – Scraps

dark-medium

light-medium

dark-medium

light-medium

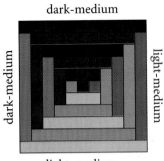

light-medium

First one made.

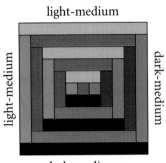

light-medium

dark-medium

light-medium

dark-medium

Second one made. The left hand side must match up with the right hand side of first block.

This one is a real challenge – I lived every minute of making this one (masochistic?) No live person should be around you (TV person is okay.) You will join the large club of people who talk aloud – alone.

Refer to page 56 for more information on these side blocks.

For this quilt, the strips were cut 1¼". Finished size is 32" x 40" plus floating.

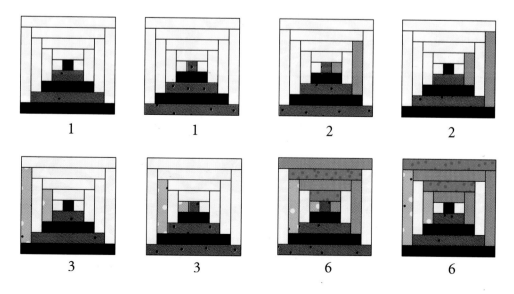

1

1

2

2

3

3

6

6

Another Courthouse Step

If you just love the fabrics you're using – keep right on making those blocks – and you can have a second quilt that looks totally different. Look ahead to page 58.

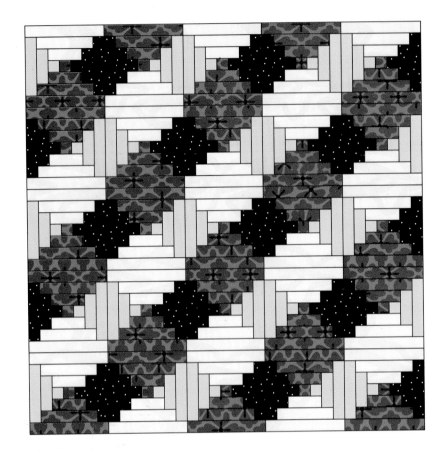

Pat Howard
Los Angeles, CA

Shaded Trails

#183, page 59, "It's Okay..."

Donna Agnelly of Waterford, WI, created an absolutely stunning quilt using this pattern as her guide. Her efforts were so successful that she won first place in the It's Okay Quilt Sitter Challenge in 1990. Attracting an international lineup of entries, requirements for the competition were few, but specific:

> Contestants had to select a pattern, or variation of one, found in any of the author's quilting books.

> Special limited edition production star fabric, designed personally by Mary Ellen, had to appear prominently in the finished works

While she was admiring the winning quilt as it hung on a wall of the Palace Station in Las Vegas, Pat Farace (Warren, NJ) exclaimed she saw spools. Jan Krueger (Hales Corners, WI) shared Pat's amazement and set out to expand on the theme. The result was Four Times Four Spools shown below.

That's what it's all about friends. Quilt design, like all forms of creative expression, is a process of evolution. What you see today certainly is exciting and beautiful; but it's only a hint of the great things that are sure to emerge tomorrow. And so, the block goes on and on...

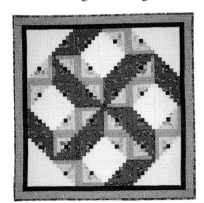

See why a progression works. We start out with a 6-patch Shaded Trails (left) exactly like the design in the "It's Okay..." book. Then we take a baby step to the next photo.

In this progression (right) is the same pattern, only re-shaded. Now, let's take a GIANT step.

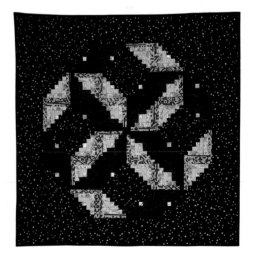

Woops looky here! Can you believe this is the same basic Shaded Trails block?

Courthouse Steps – Checkered Plaids
(visually large & small)

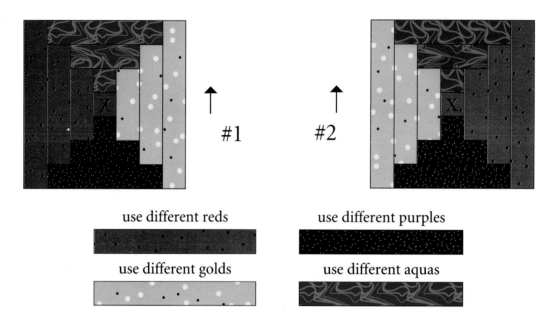

#1   #2

use different reds   use different purples

use different golds   use different aquas

1↑	2↑	1↑	2↑	1↑
1↓	2↓	1↓	2↓	1↓
1↑	2↑	1↑	2↑	1↑
1↓	2↓	1↓	2↓	1↓
1↑	2↑	1↑	2↑	1↑

NOTE: The outside red strip of Block #1 should be a different red than the outside red of Block#2. (Same with the outside strips of the aquas, golds, and purples.)

Beginning center square is marked with an X so you can see where to start – however, it should be the same fabric as in all blocks.

pieced by Kaye England
Carmel, IN

quilted by Alice Cunningham
Carmel, IN

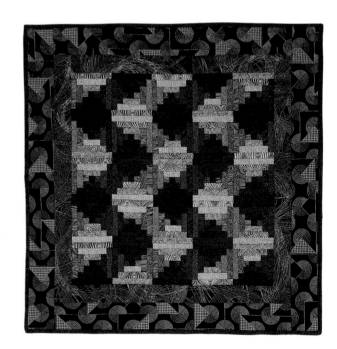

Courthouse Steps – Checkered Plaids

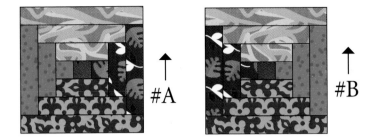

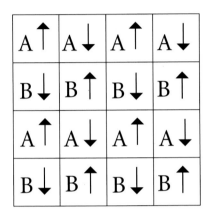

Two 4-color combinations:
One on straight.
One on diagonal.

Strips are CUT 1¼" – nice small block makes a beautiful pattern.

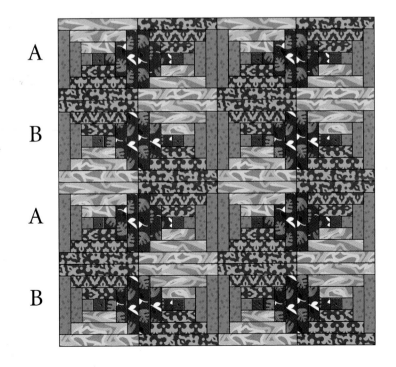

Puzzling Plaid

Plaid with three different sizes.

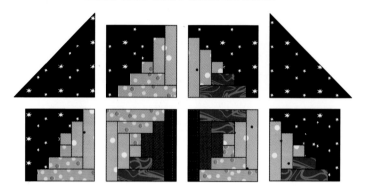

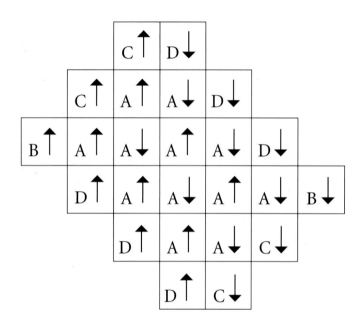

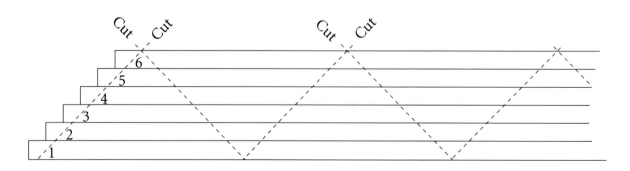

Sew long strips together to make "yardage" to cut your side half blocks. (It will look and lay better next to your Log cabin blocks.)

If strips are cut 1¼" wide, this will be approximately 20½" x 26" at this point. This design takes braids beautifully.

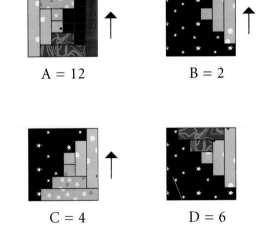

A = 12

B = 2

C = 4

D = 6

Carol Boyce
Goleta, CA

Shaded Mountains

You'll need left-hand side blocks and right-hand side blocks.

Left Block   Right Block

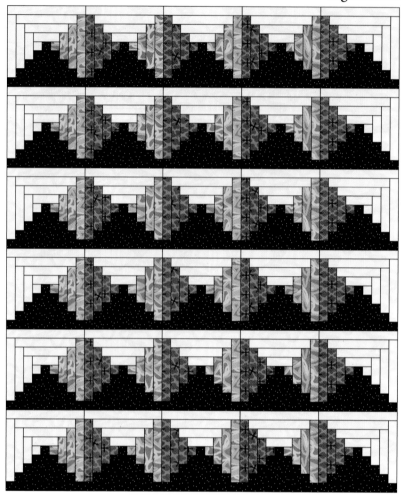

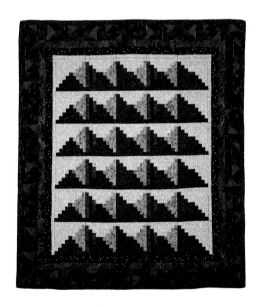

Left Block   Right Block

Refer to page 52 for
another layout using
these same blocks.

Center Block

Pat Howard
Los Angeles, CA

Down by the Border

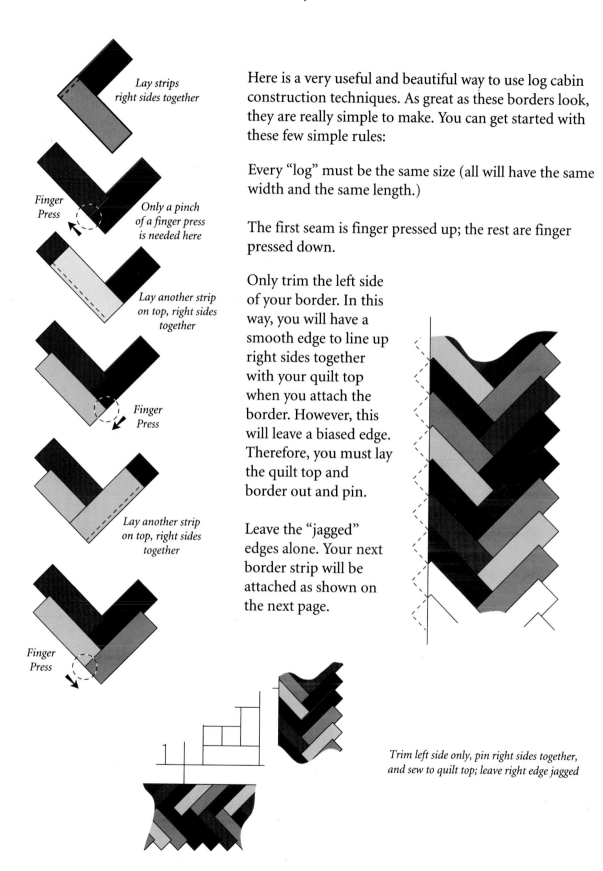

*Lay strips
right sides together*

*Finger
Press*

*Only a pinch
of a finger press
is needed here*

*Lay another strip
on top, right sides
together*

*Finger
Press*

*Lay another strip
on top, right sides
together*

*Finger
Press*

Here is a very useful and beautiful way to use log cabin construction techniques. As great as these borders look, they are really simple to make. You can get started with these few simple rules:

Every "log" must be the same size (all will have the same width and the same length.)

The first seam is finger pressed up; the rest are finger pressed down.

Only trim the left side of your border. In this way, you will have a smooth edge to line up right sides together with your quilt top when you attach the border. However, this will leave a biased edge. Therefore, you must lay the quilt top and border out and pin.

Leave the "jagged" edges alone. Your next border strip will be attached as shown on the next page.

*Trim left side only, pin right sides together,
and sew to quilt top; leave right edge jagged*

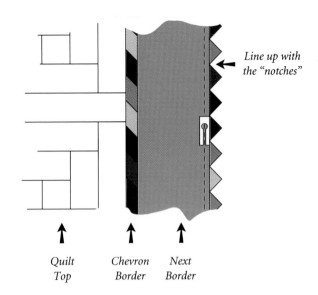

Line up with the "notches" ←

↑ | ↑ | ↑
Quilt Top | *Chevron Border* | *Next Border*

When adding borders to the chevron border, lay the next border on top of the chevron border, right sides together. Align the edge of the next border fabric with the "notches" along the "jagged" edge of the chevron border. You can trim the jagged edges *after* sewing on the border strip.

Additional borders are added in the traditional way. If you wish to add additional chevron borders outside of a "regular" border, simply do the same as when you added the chevron border to the quilt top. If you wish to add a chevron border to a chevron border, you can use the technique shown in the following section, *Bunkhouse Quilts*.

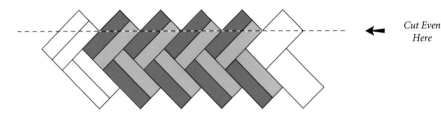

← *Cut Even Here* →

Braids, Plaits and Herringbones

Two strips sewn together and cut into rectangles make a double braid. Or, if you could simply use a striped fabric, you can cut off rectangles to get the same effect.

Three strips sewn together can cut across into rectangles make a triple braid.

The construction of the borders using these rectangles is exactly the same as for the chevron border on the previous page.

NOTE #1: Middle strip must always be a weak sister, a sitter-backer, a medium value fabric.

NOTE #2: To get the "herringbone" effect, you must always be working on either the light or dark strip.

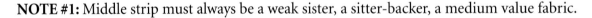

Cut Even Here ↙

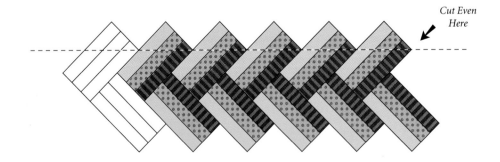

The Bunkhouse Quilt

Now, this same chevron construction technique can be used to make a whole quilt top – what I call the Bunkhouse Quilt. There are some additional construction requirements and color considerations for this quilt top.

For fabric values, the chevron strip sets must have some contrast between the left and right hand sides. You should include a few opposite contrast fabrics on each side to keep it interesting. If the contrast is too high, you will end up with just a wide dark band and a wide light band. Be sure to include mediums on both sides. Note that you must make two kinds of chevron strip sets: darker on the left side, lighter on the right; and lighter on the left, darker on the right. You just don't know how many people have made all their chevron strip sets only to find they need another bunch and they end up having to make two quilts!

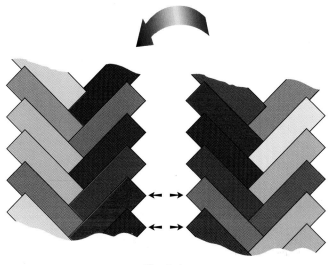

*Align Points
and lay right sides together*

The construction requirements are simple. To sew two strip sets together, make sure the adjacent fabrics are of the same value (dark to dark or light to light) and lay them right sides together. Also make sure that the points of the rectangles in the strip sets line up with each other.

While sewing, keep the edge of your sewing foot along an imaginary line connecting the inside corners (notches) where the rectangles making up the strip sets start to overlap.

Important Note: *DO NOT trim the jagged edges of the strip sets before sewing them together!*

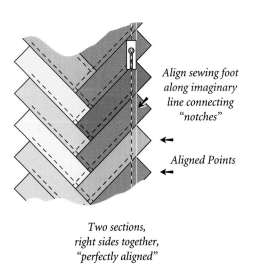

*Align sewing foot
along imaginary
line connecting
"notches"*

Aligned Points

*Two sections,
right sides together,
"perfectly aligned"*

Strip A   Strip B

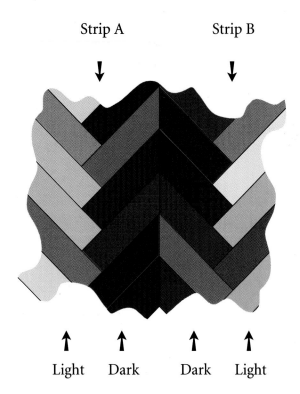

Light   Dark   Dark   Light

The completed Bunkhouse Quilt will have alternating chevrons of dark and light fabrics. Again, I must emphasize the importance of including some lights in the darks and vice-versa. Although this might not seem intuitively pleasing, it gives the quilt additional character and is pleasing to the eye.

We finish this quilt with borders in much the same way as we attach additional borders to the chevron border. Note that the attachment of the binding to the chevron will be done the same way as we attached the strip sets for the Bunkhouse Quilt here.

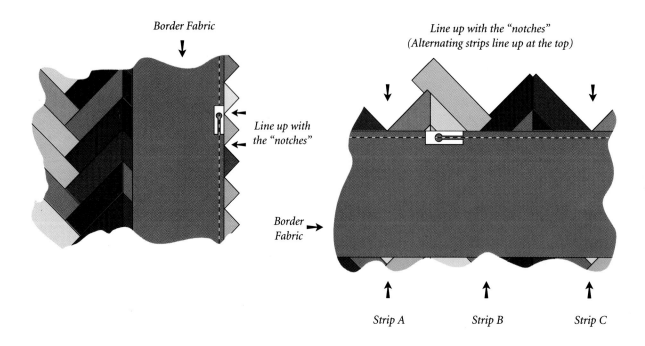

You need one other piece of information to attach the binding for the Bunkhouse Quilt. The binding at the top and bottom is attached by laying the right sides together with the border fabric aligned with the "notches" created where the dark and light fabrics come together to form the chevrons.

Harriet Berk
Santa Barbara, CA
Bunkhouse Quilt

Additional Notes

1. To re-create those wonderful antique Log Cabin quilts made from vibrant strips of silks and velvets, that were cut tiny, tiny – you'll have to do "laid work". That means sewing the strips down on a background fabric that is very light weight. This keeps the strips from fraying apart. Remember, taffeta is the first to go (wear out.)

2. Try anything – no matter how weird or strange it seems. (If it doesn't work, keep your mouth shut!)

3. I hope during August and September, 1990, that you pieced and appliqued a tiny Kuwaiti flag on the back of every quilt you were currently working on.

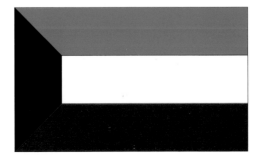

Mary Ellen Hopkins
Santa Monica, CA
Courthouse Steps
(found on page 51)

Final Message

RECYCLE – Otherwise our grandchildren may not have room to store half of that fabric we are buying today.